PRINCEWILL LAGANG

Together for Eternity: Christian Marriage and Beyond

First published by PRINCEWILL LAGANG 2023

Copyright © 2023 by Princewill Lagang

All rights reserved. No part of this publication may be reproduced, stored or transmitted in any form or by any means, electronic, mechanical, photocopying, recording, scanning, or otherwise without written permission from the publisher. It is illegal to copy this book, post it to a website, or distribute it by any other means without permission.

Princewill Lagang asserts the moral right to be identified as the author of this work.

First edition

This book was professionally typeset on Reedsy.
Find out more at reedsy.com

Contents

1	Together for Eternity: Christian Marriage and Beyond	1
2	The Foundation of Faith	4
3	The Power of Love	7
4	Nurtured by Community	10
5	Navigating Challenges and Triumphs	13
6	Growing in Faith and Love	16
7	Passing the Torch	19
8	Impacting the World	22
9	Reflecting on a Life Well-Lived	25
10	Eternal Togetherness	28
11	A Journey of Hope	31
12	The Final Amen	33

1

Together for Eternity: Christian Marriage and Beyond

In the soft glow of the morning sun, the church doors opened with a gentle creak. The congregation hushed, their breaths held in anticipation, as the bridal march began to play. All eyes turned to the back of the aisle, where Sarah stood, her heart racing and her palms moist. Clutching a bouquet of delicate white lilies, she took her father's arm, and together, they walked toward the altar.

This was the beginning of Sarah and John's journey, a sacred covenant in the eyes of God, a Christian marriage. But it was also much more than that. It was the beginning of their adventure into the eternity of togetherness, a journey through life's ups and downs, guided by their faith, love, and a shared commitment.

A Foundation of Faith

For many Christians, marriage is more than a social contract; it is a sacred covenant that reflects the profound relationship between Christ and His Church. Ephesians 5:25-33 reminds us that husbands are to love their wives as Christ loved the Church and wives to submit to their husbands as the Church submits to Christ. This deep spiritual connection serves as the foundation upon which Christian marriages are built.

Within the walls of the church, the marriage ceremony unfolds as a celebration of faith and love. Family and friends gather to witness the union, offering their blessings and support. The pastor, standing before the altar, offers words of wisdom and guidance drawn from the Bible, emphasizing the gravity and sanctity of the vows about to be exchanged.

Vows of Commitment

At the heart of every Christian marriage is the exchange of vows. These promises are more than just words; they are a solemn commitment to love and cherish one another, through all of life's trials and tribulations.

The bride and groom stand face to face, hearts open, and voices unwavering as they declare their love and fidelity. These vows bind them in unity, forming an unbreakable covenant before God. In the presence of the congregation, they pledge to support one another, to stand by each other's side in sickness and health, in joy and sorrow, for better or for worse.

Beyond the Ceremony

The wedding ceremony, although beautiful and significant, is merely the beginning. Christian marriage extends far beyond the moment when two individuals become one in the eyes of God. It is a journey filled with blessings and challenges, laughter and tears.

The Christian couple embarks on this lifelong journey with the understanding that their union is not only about the years they spend together on Earth but extends into eternity. Their love is a reflection of Christ's love for His Church – selfless, sacrificial, and unending.

As Sarah and John stood before the altar, they knew that their love was deeply rooted in their faith. Their marriage was a reflection of the love of their Creator, and their faith was the cornerstone upon which their relationship was built.

Conclusion

In this first chapter, we have delved into the heart of Christian marriage, exploring its spiritual significance, the exchange of vows, and the commitment that extends far beyond the wedding ceremony. For Sarah and John, this was just the beginning of a journey that would be filled with joy, challenges, and the unending promise to walk hand in hand, together for eternity. In the chapters that follow, we will delve deeper into the various aspects of Christian marriage, exploring the role of faith, love, and community in building a strong and enduring union.

2

The Foundation of Faith

As Sarah and John began their journey of Christian marriage, they understood that faith was not just a component of their relationship; it was the very foundation upon which they built their life together. In this chapter, we delve deeper into the role of faith in a Christian marriage, exploring how it shapes their beliefs, values, and the way they navigate the challenges of life.

Faith as the Cornerstone

For Christian couples, faith is not merely a shared interest or a common hobby; it is the cornerstone upon which their relationship is built. Their faith in God, their commitment to Jesus Christ, and their trust in the Holy Spirit guide their actions and decisions. This faith provides a sense of purpose and direction, helping them navigate the complexities of life.

In their daily lives, Sarah and John often turn to their faith as a source of strength and inspiration. They read the Bible together, pray for guidance, and seek solace in their shared beliefs. Their faith is not just an abstract concept; it is a living, breathing presence in their marriage.

A Strong Spiritual Connection

The spiritual connection between Christian couples goes beyond attending church services together. It is about a shared commitment to grow in faith, both individually and as a couple. They encourage one another in their spiritual journeys, supporting each other in times of doubt and celebrating moments of spiritual growth.

Prayer is a powerful tool for Sarah and John. They pray together for their marriage, their family, and their friends. They also pray for wisdom and strength to face life's challenges. In moments of joy, they offer prayers of gratitude, recognizing that their blessings are gifts from a loving God.

Faith and Decision-Making

Faith influences every decision they make. Whether it's a career choice, a financial decision, or a move to a new city, Sarah and John seek guidance through prayer and reflection. They trust that their faith will lead them in the right direction, even when the path is uncertain.

Their faith also shapes their values and priorities. They prioritize love, forgiveness, and kindness, mirroring the teachings of Jesus. Their values serve as a compass, helping them make ethical and moral choices that honor their faith.

Overcoming Challenges

Christian marriages are not immune to challenges. In fact, like any other marriage, they encounter difficulties, both external and internal. But it is their faith that often helps them weather these storms. They turn to God for guidance and strength, leaning on their faith to find solutions and heal wounds.

For Sarah and John, their faith is a source of hope and resilience in the face of adversity. They find solace in knowing that they are not alone in their struggles, as God is with them every step of the way.

Conclusion

In Chapter 2, we have explored the profound role of faith in Christian marriage. Faith is not just a shared belief; it is the bedrock upon which every decision, action, and thought is based. For Sarah and John, their faith is a guiding light, helping them navigate the complexities of life, make ethical choices, and find strength in moments of joy and adversity. In the chapters that follow, we will delve into the ways in which love and community further enrich their Christian marriage journey.

3

The Power of Love

In this chapter, we delve into the profound significance of love within a Christian marriage. Love is not just an emotion; it's a calling, a commitment, and a force that guides the daily lives of Sarah and John as they journey together in their Christian marriage.

Agape Love

Within Christian marriage, the love shared by the couple is often referred to as "agape" love. This love, as described in the Bible, is selfless and sacrificial. It mirrors the love that Christ has for His Church. For Sarah and John, this form of love serves as the cornerstone of their relationship.

Agape love means putting each other's needs above their own. It's a love that is unwavering, even in the face of challenges. Sarah and John strive to love each other with the same selflessness and devotion that God shows to His people.

Unconditional Commitment

Christian love is not subject to the whims of emotion or circumstance. It's an unwavering commitment to each other's well-being and spiritual growth.

For Sarah and John, love means standing by one another's side through thick and thin, for better or for worse.

Their love is unconditional and unshakable, just as God's love for His children is unwavering. This commitment is reflected in their daily actions and the decisions they make in their marriage.

Love as a Healer

Love is a powerful force that can mend wounds and heal the soul. When disagreements or misunderstandings arise, Sarah and John turn to love as a means of reconciliation. Forgiveness and empathy are central to their Christian marriage, as they understand that love can bridge any gap.

They often recall 1 Corinthians 13:4-7, a passage that describes love's attributes: "Love is patient, love is kind. It does not envy, it does not boast, it is not proud. It does not dishonor others, it is not self-seeking, it is not easily angered, it keeps no record of wrongs. Love does not delight in evil but rejoices with the truth. It always protects, always trusts, always hopes, always perseveres."

Strengthened by Love

Their love for one another is also a source of strength and courage. When faced with life's trials and tribulations, Sarah and John find solace and determination in their love. Their love propels them forward, helping them overcome obstacles, and find joy in the midst of challenges.

A Love That Reflects God's Love

In a Christian marriage, the love shared between the couple is meant to reflect God's love for humanity. It's a love that seeks to uplift and edify one another, growing in faith together. As Sarah and John journey through their marriage, their love serves as a testimony to the boundless love of God.

Conclusion

Chapter 3 explores the transformative power of love within a Christian marriage. Agape love, commitment, and the ability to heal and strengthen are at the core of Sarah and John's relationship. Their love is not merely an emotion; it's a reflection of God's love for His children and a guiding force that shapes their journey together. In the chapters that follow, we will explore how their Christian community further enriches and supports their marriage.

4

Nurtured by Community

Christian marriage isn't a solitary journey. It thrives within a broader community of faith. In this chapter, we explore how Sarah and John's Christian community enriches and supports their marriage, providing the essential backdrop against which their love and faith can flourish.

A Spiritual Support System

The Christian community plays a significant role in Sarah and John's marriage. It's a source of guidance, encouragement, and accountability. Within their church and fellowship, they find mentors and fellow believers who offer insights into married life, helping them grow in their faith and love.

Couples' Bible study groups and marriage enrichment programs are common elements within their community. These provide valuable opportunities for them to learn, share, and grow together, seeking wisdom from experienced mentors and strengthening their relationship.

Praying Together

Prayer is a fundamental aspect of Sarah and John's life within the Christian community. They engage in communal prayers, seeking divine guidance for their marriage and family. This shared spiritual practice binds them to other couples, fostering a sense of unity and collective support.

Their church community often holds special prayer sessions for married couples, where they can lay their concerns and hopes before God. It's a chance to draw strength from the collective faith of the congregation.

Mentorship and Counseling

Within their Christian community, Sarah and John have access to couples who have walked the path of Christian marriage for many years. These seasoned couples serve as mentors, offering guidance, insight, and practical advice.

When they encounter challenges within their marriage, they also have the option of seeking professional Christian counseling within their church or fellowship. These counselors provide them with a faith-based perspective on resolving conflicts and strengthening their relationship.

Celebrating Milestones and Anniversaries

Within the Christian community, milestones and anniversaries take on added significance. Sarah and John are often encouraged to celebrate their marriage in the presence of their church family. These celebrations provide an opportunity to give thanks for the journey they've undertaken together and to seek blessings for the years ahead.

Accountability and Support

Accountability is a vital aspect of their Christian community. Sarah and John are open to sharing their joys and challenges with their fellow believers, who provide prayer, advice, and support. This sense of accountability encourages them to uphold their commitment to their marriage and faith.

Conclusion

Chapter 4 explores how the Christian community serves as a nurturing environment for Sarah and John's marriage. Within this community, they find spiritual support, guidance, and mentorship. They share their faith and love with fellow believers, drawing strength from the collective wisdom and encouragement. In the chapters that follow, we will delve deeper into how they navigate specific challenges and celebrate the milestones of their Christian marriage.

5

Navigating Challenges and Triumphs

Christian marriage is a journey filled with both challenges and triumphs. In this chapter, we explore how Sarah and John navigate the trials and tribulations of life, drawing strength from their faith and love to overcome obstacles and celebrating the victories that come their way.

Challenges: Tests of Faith and Love

Christian couples, like any others, face their share of challenges. These may come in the form of financial difficulties, health issues, conflicts, or external pressures. For Sarah and John, these challenges are seen as tests of their faith and love.

When adversity strikes, they turn to prayer and their faith to find solace and solutions. They draw on the support of their Christian community, seeking guidance and encouragement from those who have walked a similar path.

Communication: The Key to Resolution

Effective communication is an essential tool in overcoming challenges. Sarah and John understand that open, honest, and respectful communication is vital in resolving conflicts and maintaining a strong and healthy marriage. They strive to listen to one another and express their thoughts and feelings with love and understanding.

In times of disagreement, they turn to prayer and the guidance of their Christian community for advice on how to address and resolve the issue. The power of love and forgiveness often helps them mend any emotional wounds.

Seeking Professional Help

For more complex issues, they are not hesitant to seek professional help within their Christian community. Pastors, counselors, and therapists who share their faith can offer them guidance, often incorporating biblical wisdom into their advice. This support ensures that they have the tools to address even the most challenging obstacles in their marriage.

Triumphs: Celebrating Milestones and Blessings

Alongside challenges come moments of triumph and joy. Christian couples recognize the importance of celebrating milestones and blessings within their marriage. They offer prayers of gratitude and thanksgiving, acknowledging that every success is a gift from God.

Sarah and John find meaning in marking their wedding anniversaries within the Christian community, as they reflect on the journey they've taken and the love and faith that continue to strengthen their bond.

A Resilient Love

As Sarah and John navigate challenges and triumphs, they discover that their love is more resilient and enduring than they ever imagined. Their faith serves as a bedrock of strength, and their shared commitment to God's love provides them with the courage to face whatever life throws their way.

Conclusion

Chapter 5 delves into how Sarah and John navigate the challenges and celebrate the triumphs in their Christian marriage. Through faith, love, communication, and the support of their Christian community, they find the strength to overcome adversity and the humility to give thanks for their blessings. Their journey continues, marked by a love that endures all things, reflecting God's boundless love for His people. In the chapters that follow, we will explore their ongoing commitment to growing in faith and love together, knowing that their journey is one of eternal togetherness.

6

Growing in Faith and Love

In this chapter, we delve into Sarah and John's ongoing commitment to growing in faith and love within their Christian marriage. Their journey is a continuous process of deepening their spirituality, strengthening their love, and enriching their relationship.

A Shared Spiritual Journey

For Sarah and John, the journey of faith is an ongoing adventure. They continue to study the Bible together, attend church services, and participate in various spiritual activities within their Christian community. This shared spiritual journey deepens their connection and reinforces the foundation of their marriage.

Prayer and Devotion

Prayer remains a cornerstone of their daily lives. They pray together, both as a couple and with their Christian community, seeking guidance, giving thanks, and sharing their challenges. Their devotion to prayer keeps their hearts aligned with God's will and their love for each other.

Expanding Their Understanding of Faith

As they grow in their faith, Sarah and John are open to exploring new dimensions of spirituality. They delve into theological discussions, attend faith-based workshops, and read books that challenge and expand their understanding of God and His plan for their lives. This intellectual and spiritual growth enhances their connection with one another.

Service and Ministry

Their faith journey isn't limited to personal growth. Sarah and John actively engage in service and ministry within their Christian community. They view this as an extension of their faith, an opportunity to give back to their church, and a way to express their love for others. Serving together strengthens their bond as they share in the joy of making a positive impact.

Celebrating Milestones of Faith

Just as they celebrate milestones in their marriage, Sarah and John also mark significant milestones in their faith journey. Baptisms, confirmations, and other sacred events become moments of reflection and thanksgiving. These occasions serve as reminders of the role their faith plays in their marriage and personal growth.

Continued Commitment to Love

As they grow in faith, their love deepens. Sarah and John understand that love is not static but ever-evolving. They continue to make intentional efforts to express their love through acts of kindness, affection, and thoughtful gestures. Their commitment to love as Christ loved the Church remains unwavering.

Conclusion

Chapter 6 explores how Sarah and John's Christian marriage is a continuous journey of growth in faith and love. Their shared spiritual exploration, devotion, service, and celebration of faith milestones enrich their relationship. This ongoing commitment to deepening their spirituality and love reflects their understanding that their journey is one of eternal togetherness, bound by faith and anchored in love. In the chapters that follow, we will further explore their unwavering commitment to each other and to their shared faith.

7

Passing the Torch

As Sarah and John's Christian marriage journey unfolds, they realize that their commitment to faith and love carries with it a responsibility to pass on their wisdom and values to future generations. In this chapter, we explore how they embrace the role of mentors and parents, leaving a lasting legacy of faith, love, and commitment.

Mentorship within the Community

Sarah and John have always valued the guidance and mentorship they received from experienced couples in their Christian community. Now, they eagerly embrace the role of mentors themselves. They offer support and advice to newlyweds and young couples, sharing their own experiences, both the challenges and triumphs, to help others navigate the early stages of their own Christian marriages.

Parenting with Faith and Love

Parenting is a sacred responsibility for Sarah and John. They approach it with the same level of devotion they bring to their marriage. They strive to instill strong Christian values in their children, nurturing their spiritual growth and helping them develop a deep relationship with God.

Family Devotions

As a family, they incorporate daily devotions into their routine, reading the Bible together, praying, and discussing the scriptures. These moments of shared spirituality deepen their familial bonds and serve as a way to pass on their faith to the next generation.

Celebrating Family Milestones

Just as Sarah and John celebrate their wedding anniversaries and faith milestones, they encourage their children to do the same. Family celebrations of birthdays, baptisms, and confirmations become opportunities for their children to reflect on the significance of faith and love in their lives.

Teaching by Example

Sarah and John understand the power of leading by example. They strive to demonstrate their love, devotion, and unwavering faith in their daily lives. Their children witness their parents' commitment to faith and love, serving as an inspiring model for building strong Christian marriages of their own.

Leaving a Lasting Legacy

As they pass on their faith and values to their children, Sarah and John know that they are leaving a lasting legacy. They recognize that their marriage is not only about their personal journey but also about the impact they can have on the generations to come.

Conclusion

Chapter 7 explores how Sarah and John embrace the role of mentors and parents, passing on their wisdom, faith, and love to future generations. Their commitment to fostering strong Christian marriages and nurturing the spiritual growth of their children is a testament to their understanding of the enduring nature of Christian love. Their journey is not just for themselves but for all those who come after them, carrying forward a legacy of faith, love, and commitment. In the chapters that follow, we will delve deeper into the ways their Christian marriage continues to evolve and impact the world around them.

8

Impacting the World

As Sarah and John's Christian marriage journey continues, they recognize that their commitment to faith and love has a broader impact beyond their family and community. In this chapter, we explore how they strive to make a positive difference in the world through their marriage and shared values.

Community Outreach and Service

Sarah and John are deeply committed to giving back to their community. They actively engage in various outreach programs, supporting the less fortunate and spreading the love and compassion they've cultivated in their Christian marriage. Through these acts of service, they aim to be a living example of Christ's love to those in need.

Supporting Missions and Charities

Their faith prompts them to support missions and charities that align with their values. They contribute financially and offer their time and skills to organizations that serve both their local and global communities. By doing so, they impact the world in a meaningful and tangible way, reflecting their commitment to love and care for all of God's children.

Advocating for Social Justice

Sarah and John understand that love extends to working for social justice. They are active advocates for various social causes, such as alleviating poverty, supporting refugees, and addressing issues of injustice. Their faith motivates them to be agents of positive change in the world, standing up for the marginalized and oppressed.

Influence in the Workplace

Their values extend to their professional lives as well. Sarah and John aim to be ethical and compassionate leaders in their respective fields. They view their work as an extension of their faith, using their influence to create a positive and Christ-like impact on the organizations and communities they serve.

Mentoring and Inspiring Others

Their commitment to faith and love isn't confined to their family and friends; they seek to inspire and mentor others outside their immediate circle. They recognize the power of their Christian marriage as a testimony to the enduring nature of love and faith and actively share their journey to encourage and guide others.

Global Mission Work

Sarah and John participate in global mission work, traveling to different parts of the world to share their faith, love, and practical support. They work alongside local communities to provide education, healthcare, and spiritual guidance. Their international efforts reflect their commitment to making a positive impact on a global scale.

Conclusion

Chapter 8 explores how Sarah and John's Christian marriage extends its influence to impact the world in a positive way. Their commitment to faith, love, and their shared values drives them to serve their community, support charitable causes, advocate for social justice, and inspire others. Their marriage is not just a personal journey but a testament to the transformative power of faith and love, capable of creating a brighter and more compassionate world for all. In the chapters that follow, we will continue to explore the evolving nature of their Christian marriage and the enduring legacy they leave behind.

9

Reflecting on a Life Well-Lived

As Sarah and John enter a new phase of their Christian marriage, they find themselves reflecting on the journey they've undertaken. In this chapter, we explore the wisdom they've gained, the legacy they're leaving, and the continued growth of their faith, love, and commitment.

Gratitude and Reflection

Gratitude is at the forefront of their reflections. Sarah and John are thankful for the rich, rewarding life they've built together. They take the time to look back on the challenges they've faced, the triumphs they've celebrated, and the deep love and faith that have sustained them.

Passing Down Wisdom

Reflecting on their life together, they understand the importance of passing down the wisdom they've gained. They are eager to share their experiences, both the lessons they've learned and the joys they've experienced, with younger couples and the next generation.

Celebrating Milestones

Milestones continue to be a central part of their lives. They celebrate not only their wedding anniversaries but also the many faith-related milestones they've achieved together. These occasions serve as reminders of the enduring nature of their Christian marriage and the strength of their shared values.

Continued Growth in Faith and Love

While they've come a long way in their faith journey, Sarah and John know that there is always room for growth. They remain committed to deepening their spirituality, further expanding their understanding of love, and nurturing their faith.

Embracing Change

As they reflect on their marriage, they understand that change is a natural part of life. They embrace the changes they've gone through and anticipate the changes that lie ahead. Their unwavering faith and love give them the resilience to adapt and grow together as their Christian marriage evolves.

Leaving a Legacy

Sarah and John are acutely aware of the legacy they are leaving behind. Their Christian marriage, built on faith, love, and commitment, is a testament to the enduring nature of love. They take pride in the knowledge that they have impacted their community, inspired others, and, most importantly, raised children who carry their values forward.

Conclusion

In Chapter 9, we explore how Sarah and John find themselves reflecting on a life well-lived, filled with faith, love, and commitment. Their gratitude, wisdom, and the legacy they're leaving behind are central to their ongoing journey. Their Christian marriage continues to evolve, marked by a deepening understanding of faith and love and a commitment to inspiring and guiding others on their own paths. In the final chapter, we will explore the culmination of their Christian marriage and the eternal togetherness they've strived for.

10

Eternal Togetherness

In this final chapter of Sarah and John's journey, we explore the culmination of their Christian marriage and the concept of eternal togetherness. Their faith, love, and commitment have carried them through a lifetime of experiences, and as they approach the later years of their life, they find solace in the knowledge that their togetherness extends beyond earthly boundaries.

A Lifetime of Shared Memories

Sarah and John look back on a lifetime of shared memories. They remember the laughter and joy, the trials and tribulations, and the countless moments of love and companionship that have defined their Christian marriage. These memories are etched in their hearts, a testament to the power of love and faith.

Continued Growth and Learning

Even in their later years, Sarah and John continue to grow in faith and love. Their journey is ongoing, and they are dedicated to deepening their spiritual connection and love for each other. They find that the more they explore their faith, the more profound and meaningful their love becomes.

Passing on the Torch

As they approach the end of their earthly journey, Sarah and John are mindful of the legacy they are leaving behind. They see the impact of their faith, love, and commitment in the lives of their children and the broader community. They are grateful for the opportunity to pass on their wisdom and values to future generations.

Facing Challenges Together

Though they've encountered their share of challenges, Sarah and John have faced them together, hand in hand. Their faith has been a source of strength, and their love has been a beacon of light during the darkest times. They've learned that facing life's trials together is a testament to the enduring nature of their commitment.

Eternal Togetherness

For Sarah and John, the concept of eternal togetherness is not just a metaphor; it's a deeply held belief. They know that, as their Christian faith teaches them, their love is not confined to this earthly life. They trust that they will be reunited in the presence of God, where their love will continue to flourish for all eternity.

Conclusion

In this final chapter, we explore the concept of eternal togetherness in the context of Sarah and John's Christian marriage. Their journey, built on faith, love, and commitment, has been a lifetime of shared experiences, growth, and legacy-building. As they face the later years of their lives, they look forward to the promise of eternal togetherness, confident that their love will transcend earthly boundaries and endure for all time. Their Christian marriage is a testimony to the enduring nature of love and faith, a journey that truly lasts for eternity.

11

A Journey of Hope

Sarah and John's Christian marriage has reached a point of deep reflection and contemplation. In this chapter, we explore how their enduring faith, love, and commitment have led them to a place of profound hope, both for their eternal togetherness and the world they leave behind.

A Legacy of Love

As they journey through their later years, Sarah and John take pride in the legacy of love they've created. Their marriage has been a living example of faith and love, a testament to their commitment to God and one another. They have touched the lives of their children, their community, and others who have witnessed their journey, leaving a legacy that reflects the power of enduring love.

Hope for Future Generations

Sarah and John hold hope for future generations. They believe in the potential of young couples to embrace faith, love, and commitment in their own Christian marriages. They are optimistic about the ability of the Christian community to continue nurturing and supporting strong, enduring marriages.

Faith in Eternal Togetherness

Their faith is unwavering in the concept of eternal togetherness. They find solace in the belief that their love will continue beyond this earthly life. Their faith assures them that they will be reunited in the presence of God, where their love will flourish for all eternity.

Continued Growth in Love and Faith

Even in their later years, Sarah and John continue to experience growth in love and faith. They cherish each moment together, knowing that their journey is ongoing. They embrace the opportunity to deepen their spiritual connection and enrich their love for one another.

Hope for a Better World

Their Christian faith and the love they've cultivated fuel their hope for a better world. They pray for peace, justice, and an end to suffering, both locally and globally. They believe that their Christian community, along with others who share their faith, can be agents of positive change in the world.

Conclusion

Chapter 11 explores how Sarah and John's Christian marriage has led them to a place of profound hope. Their journey has been marked by a legacy of love, a belief in the potential of future generations, unwavering faith in eternal togetherness, and an enduring commitment to growth in love and faith. Their hope extends beyond their own lives, as they envision a world where the values of faith, love, and commitment continue to inspire and uplift others. Their Christian marriage is a testament to the enduring nature of love, a journey of hope that lasts for eternity.

12

The Final Amen

In the twilight of their Christian marriage journey, Sarah and John find themselves reflecting on the culmination of their faith, love, and commitment. In this concluding chapter, we explore the legacy they leave, the enduring nature of their togetherness, and the sense of fulfillment that accompanies a life lived in accordance with their Christian values.

A Life Well-Lived

As they approach the final chapters of their earthly journey, Sarah and John have a profound sense of fulfillment. They look back on a life well-lived, marked by unwavering faith, enduring love, and a commitment that has withstood the test of time. Their Christian marriage has been the source of immense joy and countless blessings.

Passing the Torch

They are content in the knowledge that they've passed on their wisdom and values to their children and the broader Christian community. The torch of faith, love, and commitment is in the capable hands of the next generation, and they have done their part to ensure that these values will continue to thrive.

The Legacy of Love

Their legacy is a legacy of love. Their Christian marriage serves as a model for enduring commitment, a living testament to the power of faith and love. Their journey, from the day they stood at the altar to their twilight years, has been marked by a love that has grown stronger with each passing day.

Hope for Eternal Togetherness

Sarah and John's faith provides them with hope for eternal togetherness. They believe that, as their Christian faith teaches them, they will be reunited in the presence of God. This hope is the ultimate source of comfort as they near the end of their earthly journey.

The Final Amen

Their Christian marriage is marked by a sense of finality, yet not an end. It's the closing chapter of their earthly journey, but it's also the beginning of an eternal togetherness. They offer their final amen with gratitude for the life they've shared, the love they've known, and the faith that has sustained them.

Conclusion

In this concluding chapter, we explore how Sarah and John find a sense of fulfillment in the twilight of their Christian marriage journey. Their legacy of love, their hope for eternal togetherness, and their closing amen reflect the enduring nature of faith and love. Their Christian marriage has been a testament to the transformative power of these values, a journey that truly lasts for eternity.

Title: Together for Eternity: Christian Marriage and Beyond

Book Summary:

"Together for Eternity: Christian Marriage and Beyond" is a profound exploration of a Christian couple's enduring journey through life, love, faith, and commitment. This beautifully written book provides a detailed account of Sarah and John's Christian marriage, highlighting its multifaceted dimensions and the enduring values that underpin it.

The book is structured into twelve chapters, each offering a deep dive into the various facets of Sarah and John's Christian marriage journey. It begins with their wedding day, emphasizing the significance of the marriage covenant. As the chapters progress, readers are taken on a journey through the couple's shared faith, the importance of love as a cornerstone, the role of their Christian community, and how they navigate both challenges and triumphs.

Through each chapter, the reader witnesses the couple's unwavering commitment to growing in faith and love. The book explores their roles as mentors, parents, and change-makers within their community, providing insights into how their faith and love have impacted the world around them.

The later chapters delve into the legacy they are leaving and the concept of eternal togetherness. As Sarah and John approach the later years of their life, the book reflects on the wisdom they've gained, the enduring nature of their commitment, and their hope for the future.

"Together for Eternity: Christian Marriage and Beyond" is not just a celebration of one couple's journey; it's a testament to the transformative power of faith, love, and commitment in Christian marriages. It serves as an inspiring guide for couples seeking to build enduring relationships based on these timeless values. The book beautifully captures the essence of a love that truly lasts for eternity.

www.ingramcontent.com/pod-product-compliance
Lightning Source LLC
LaVergne TN
LVHW010442070526
838199LV00066B/6143